FIND THE CORRECT SHADOW

facebook: www.facebook.com/boudissa.123boudissa

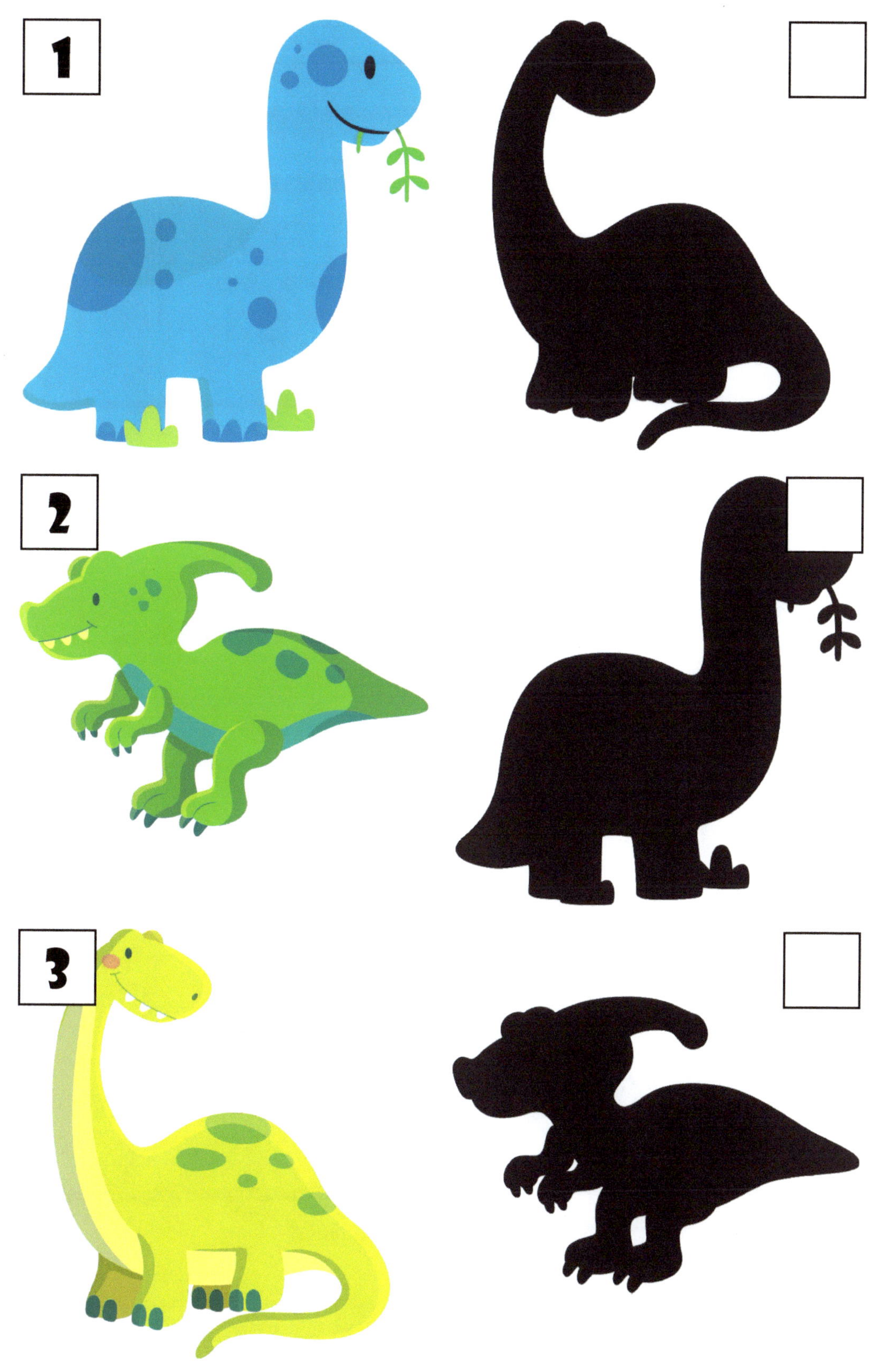

1
2
3

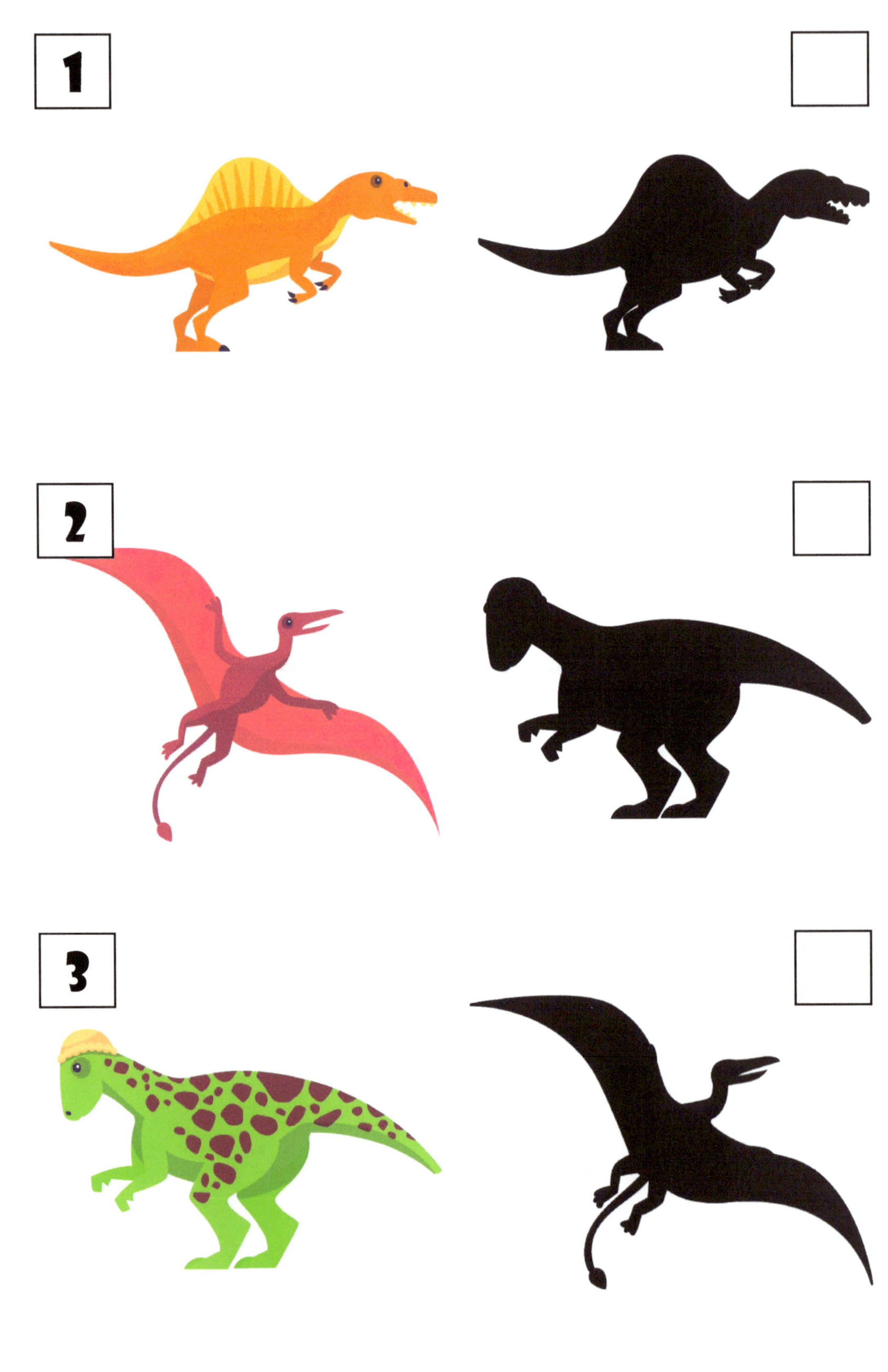

1
2
3

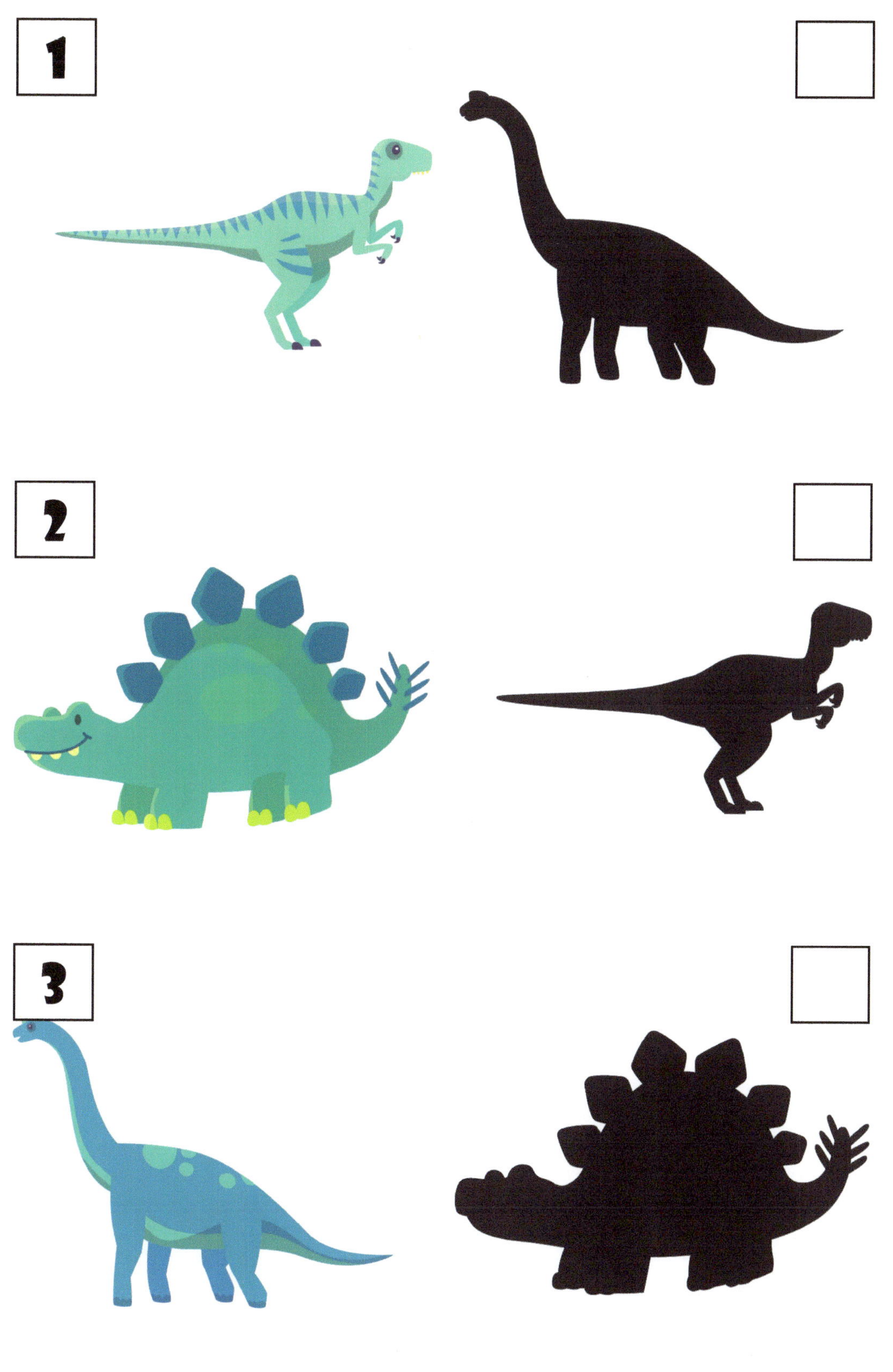

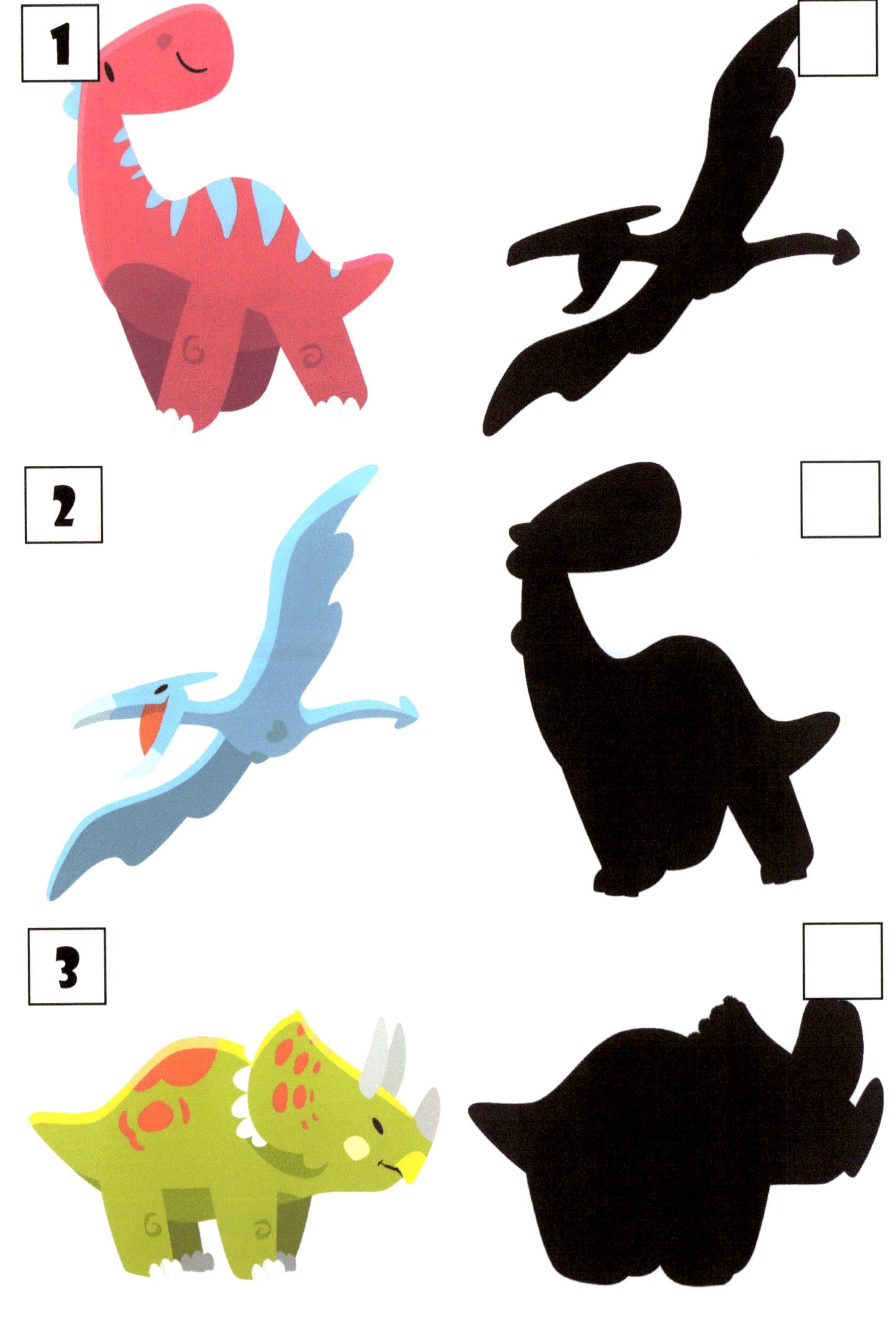

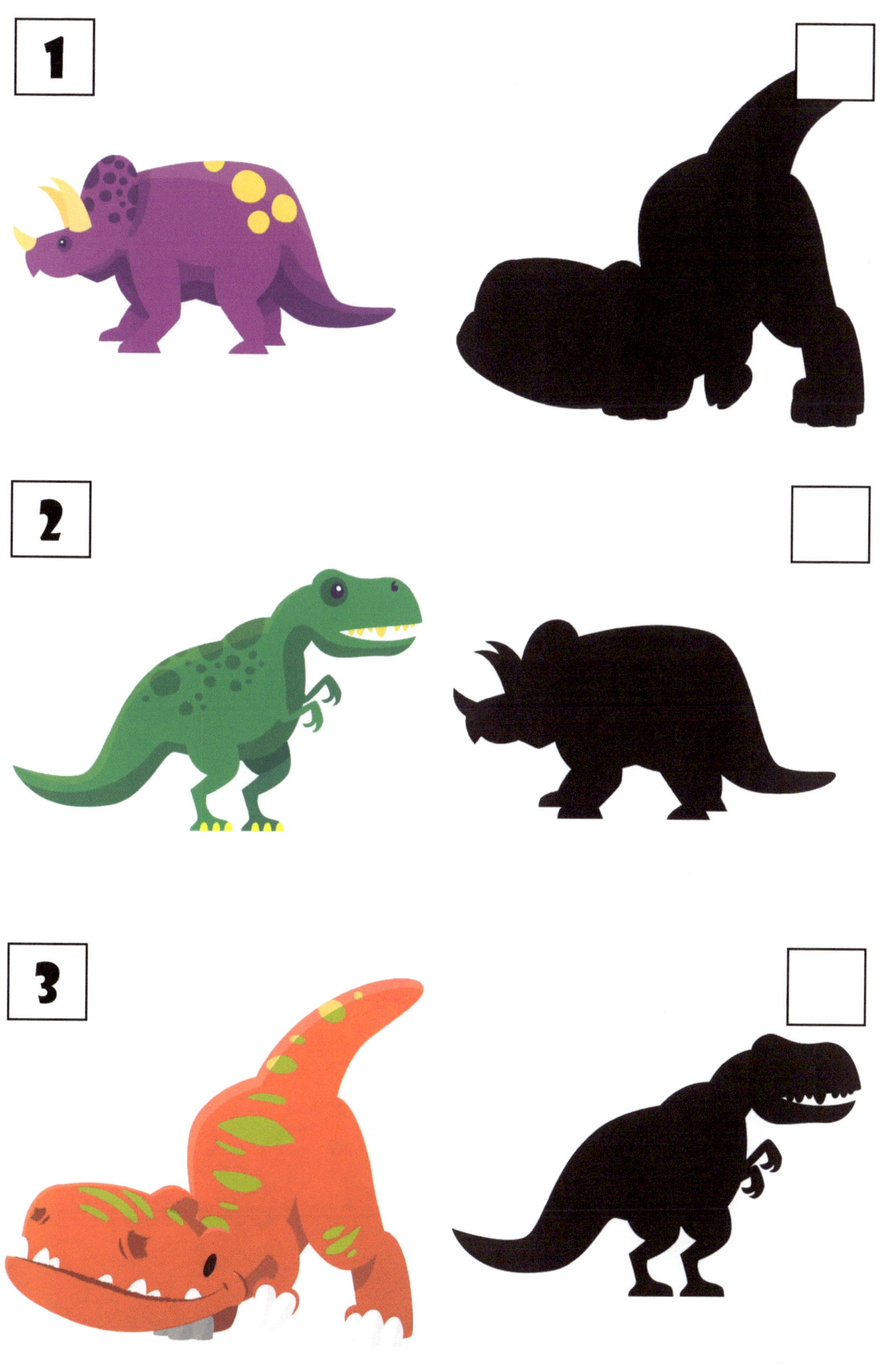

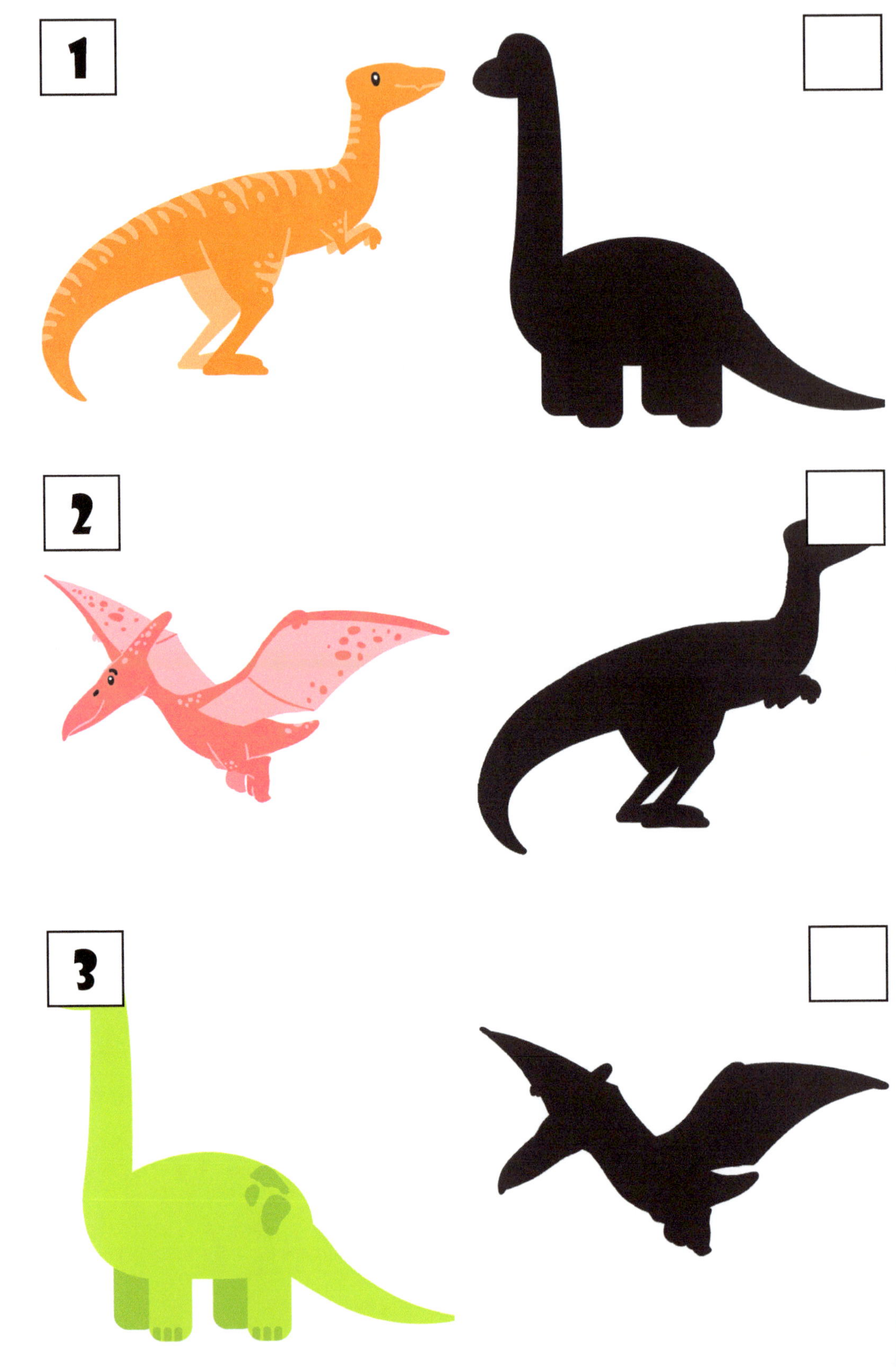

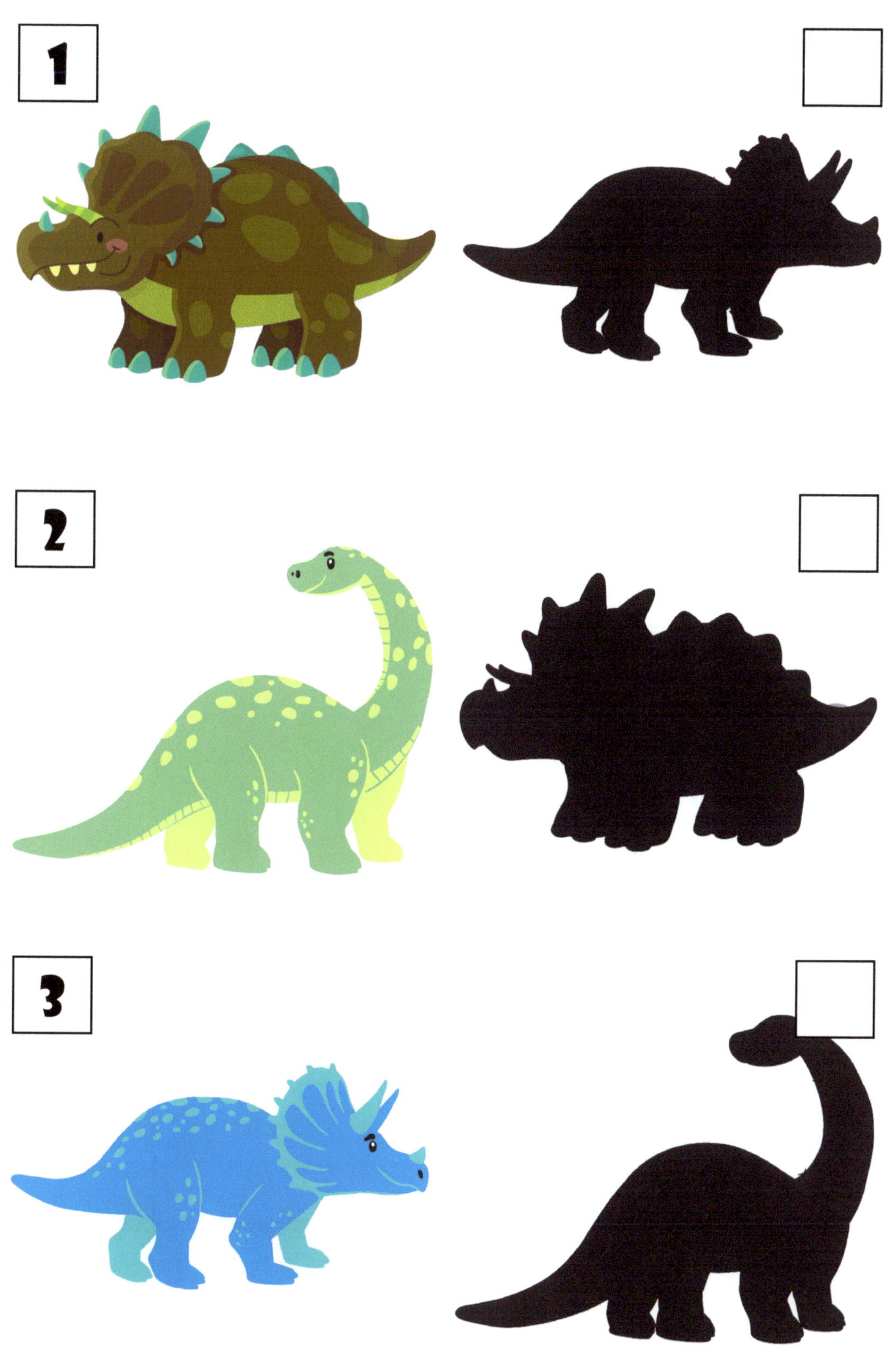

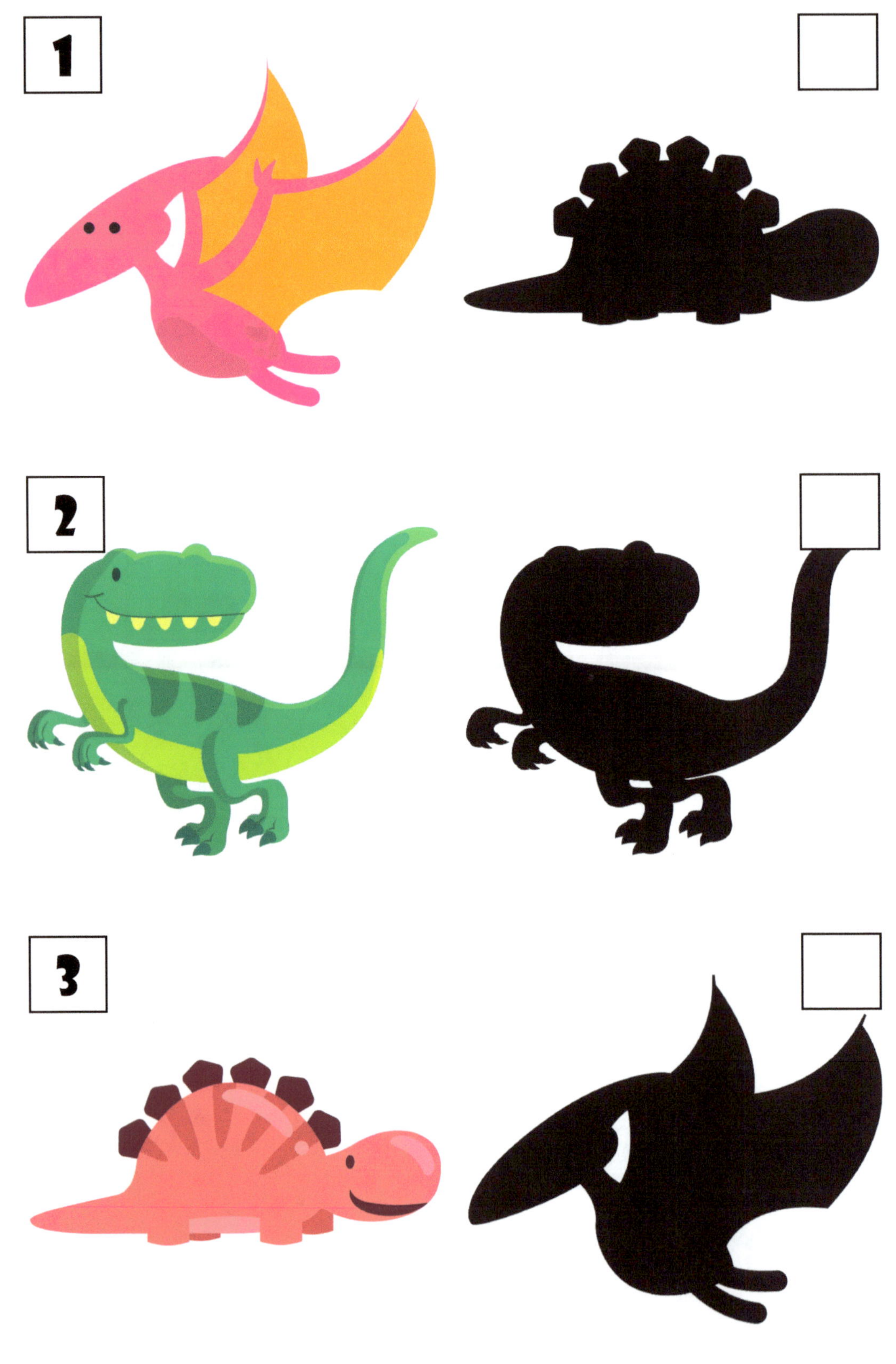

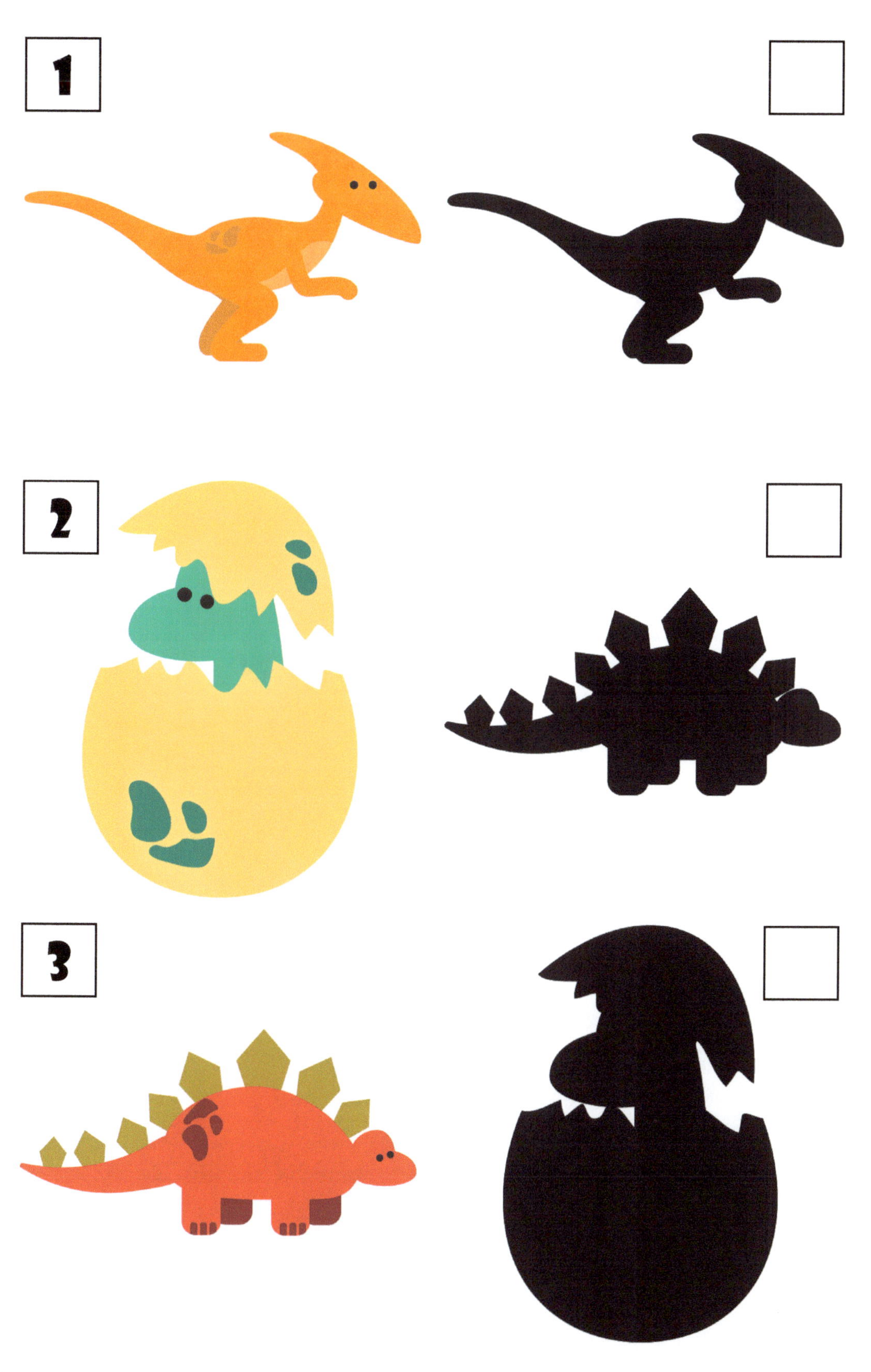

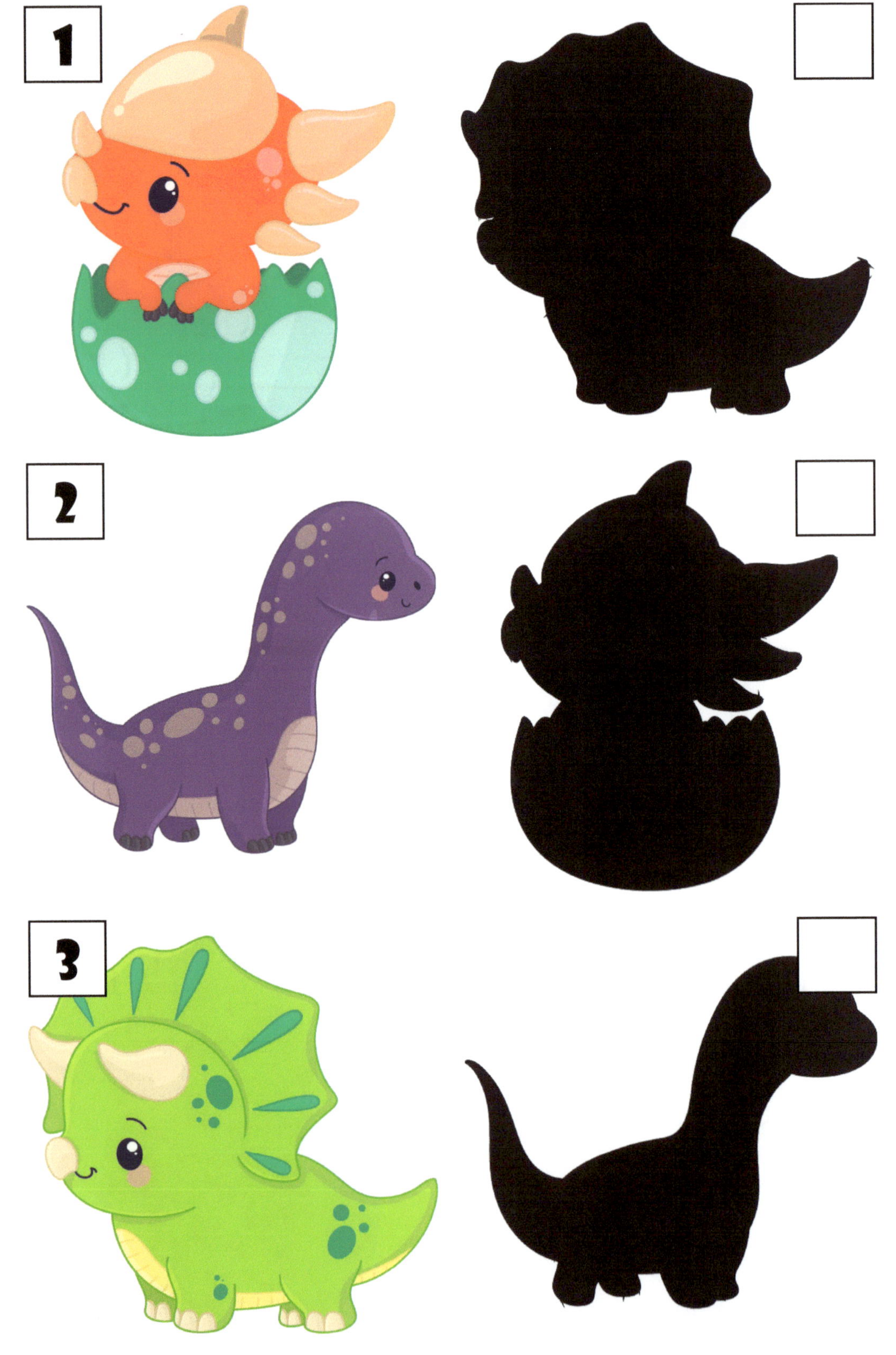

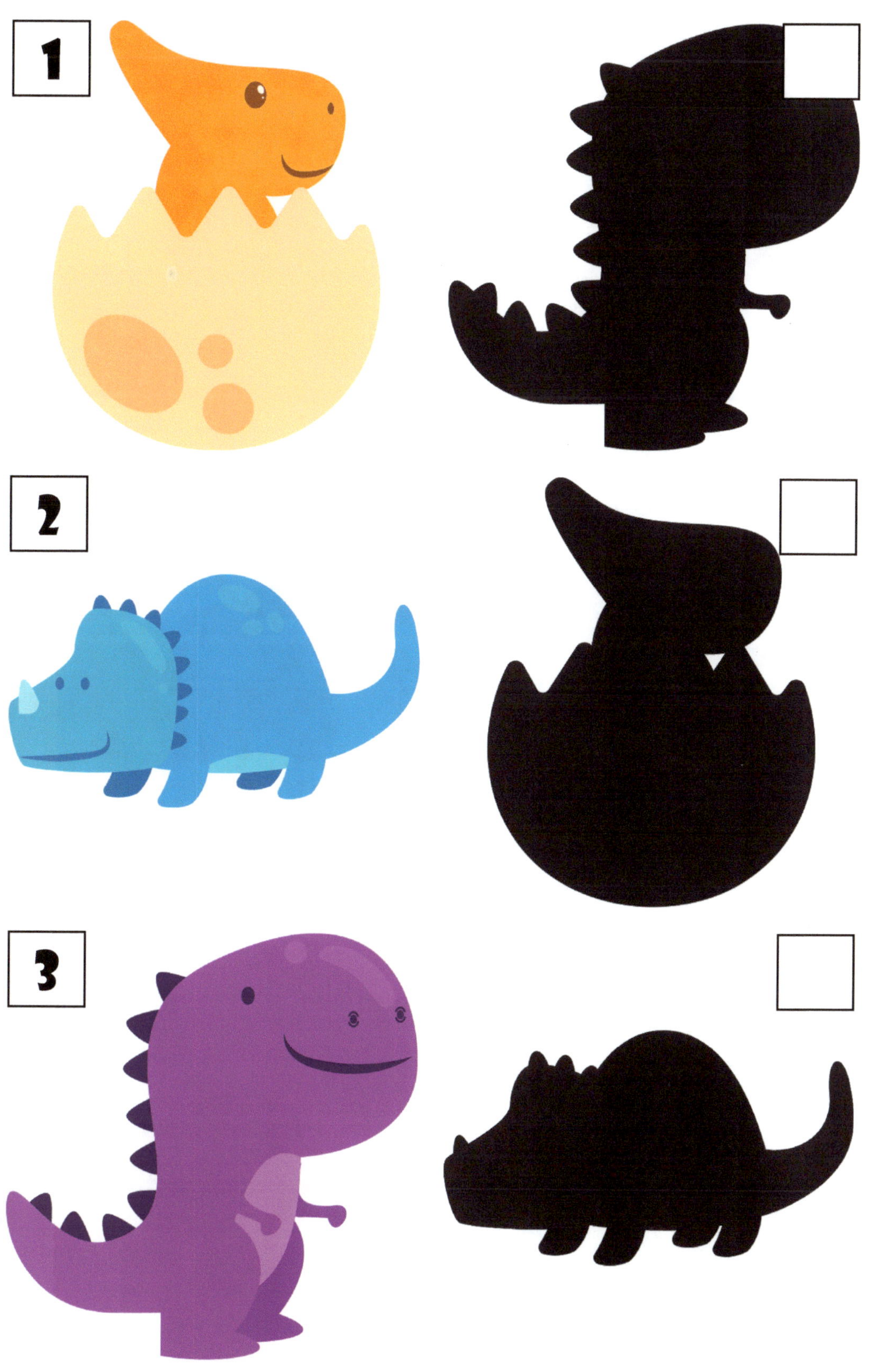

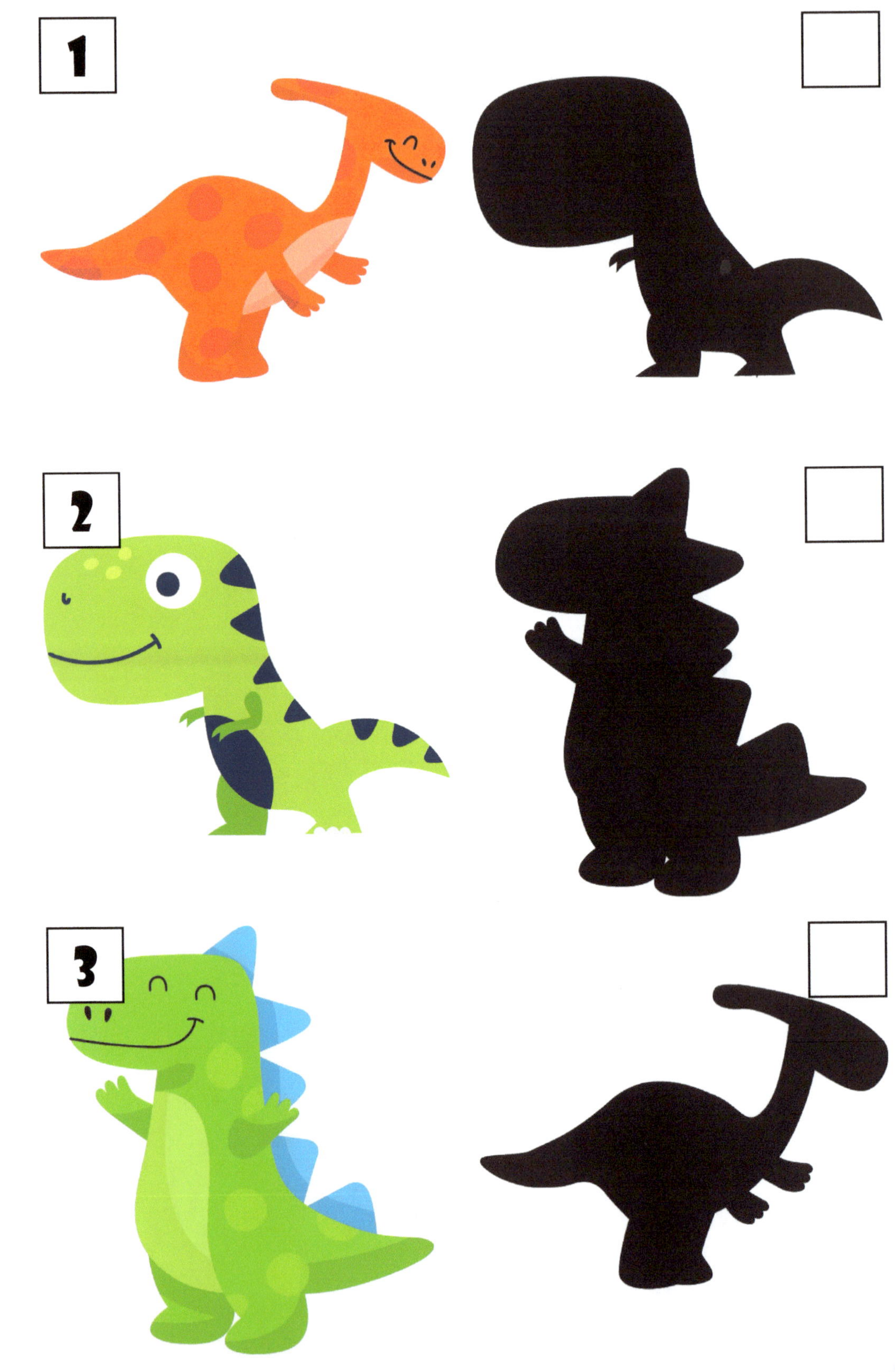

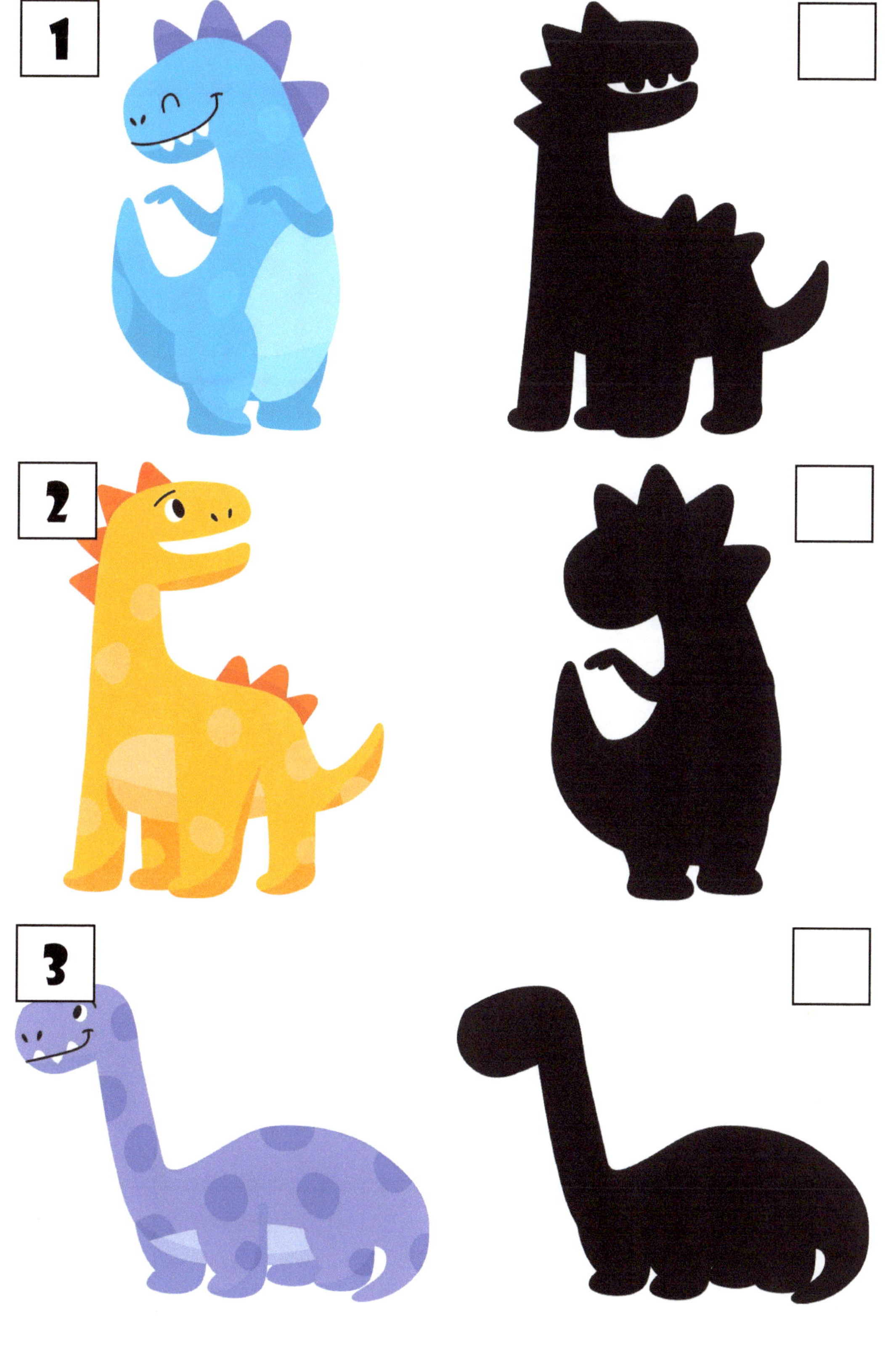

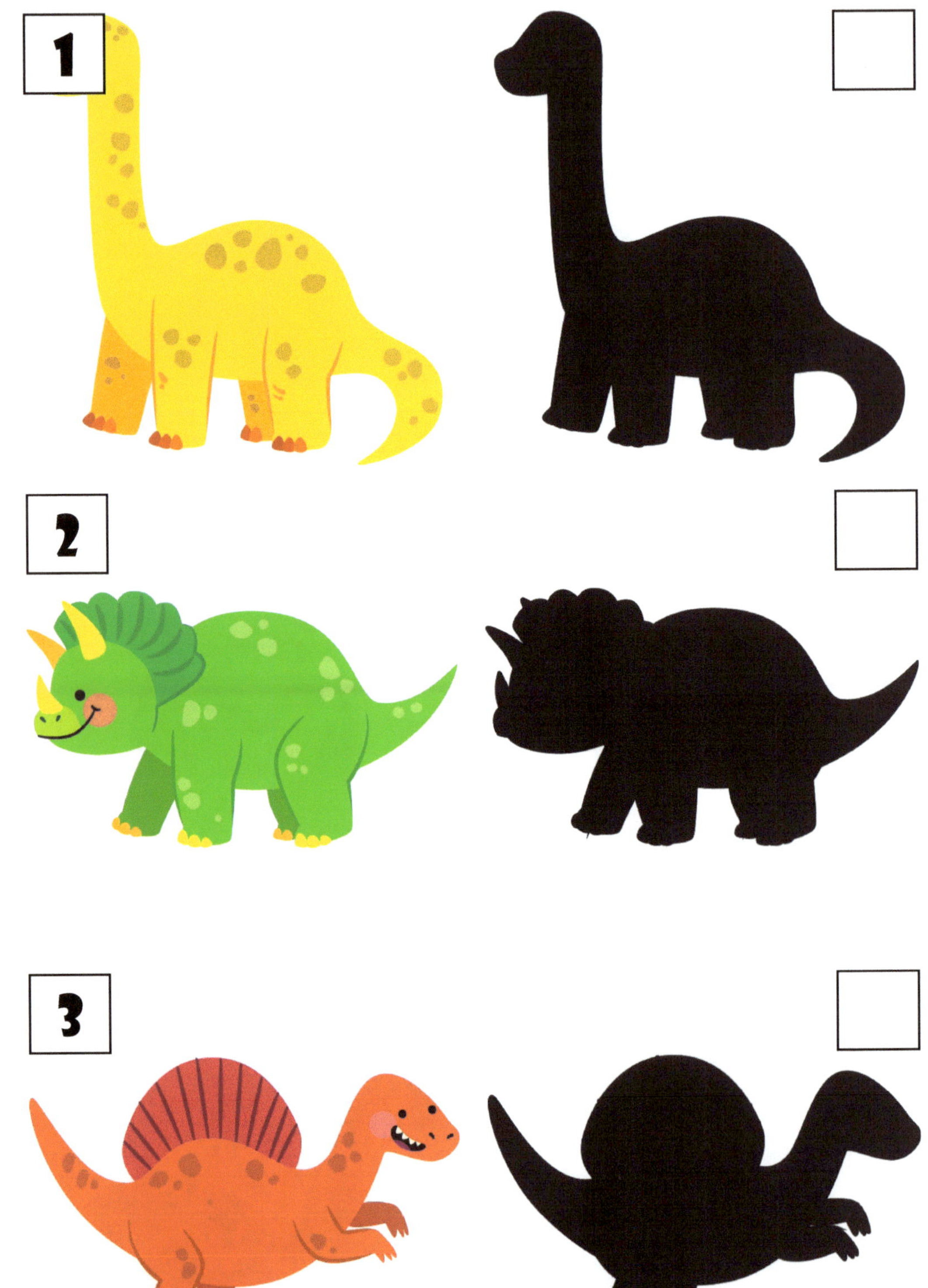

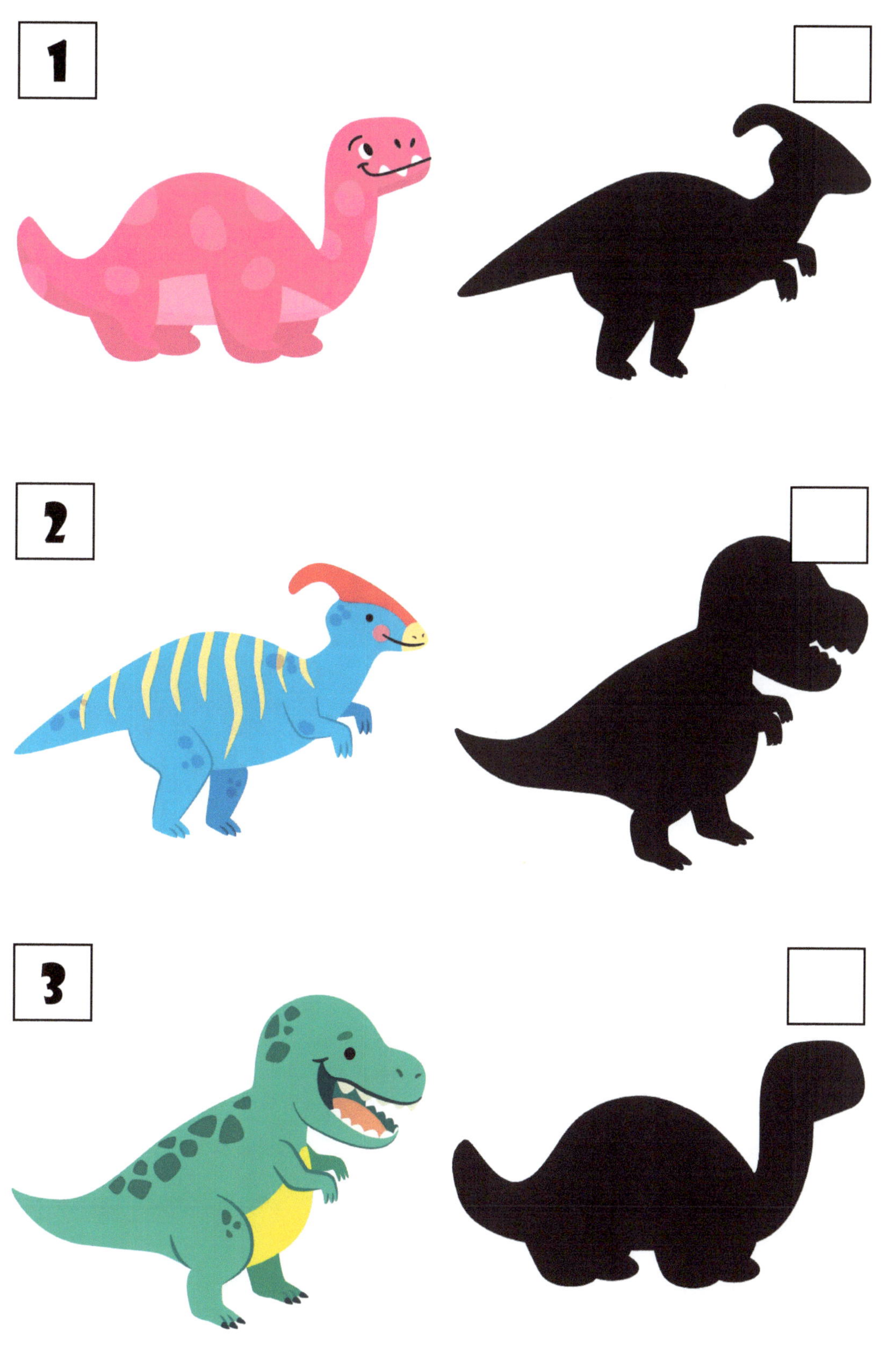

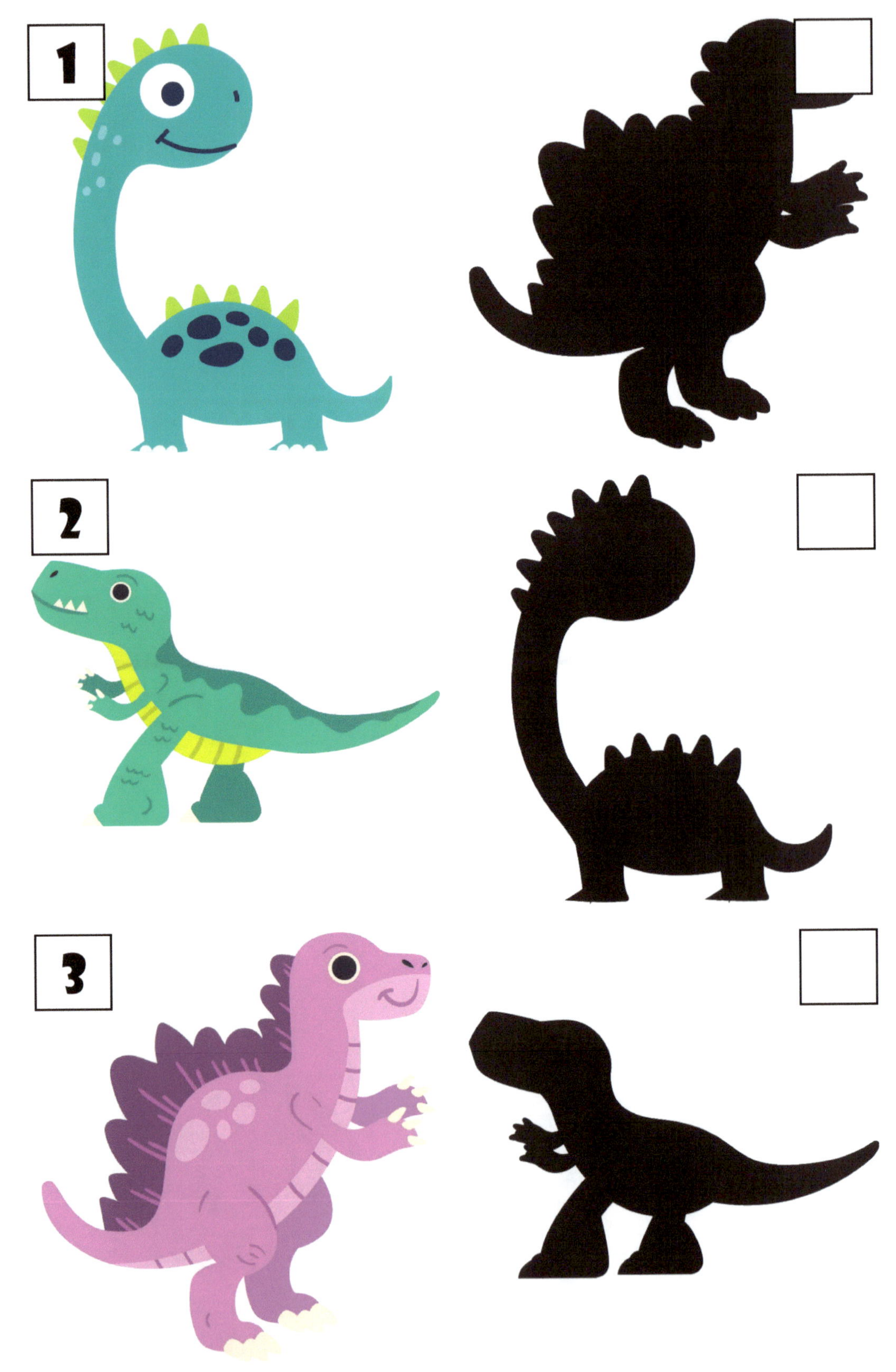

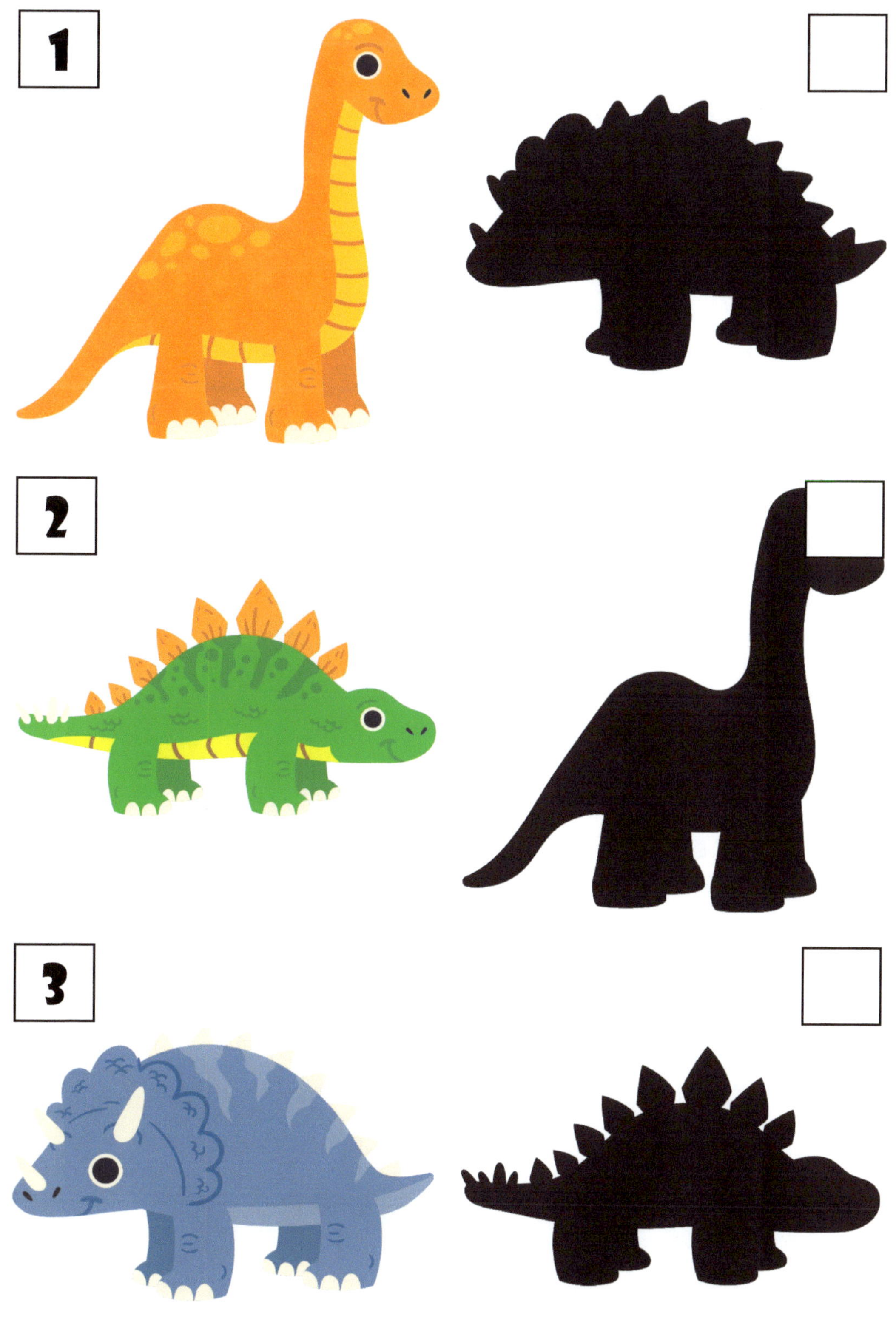

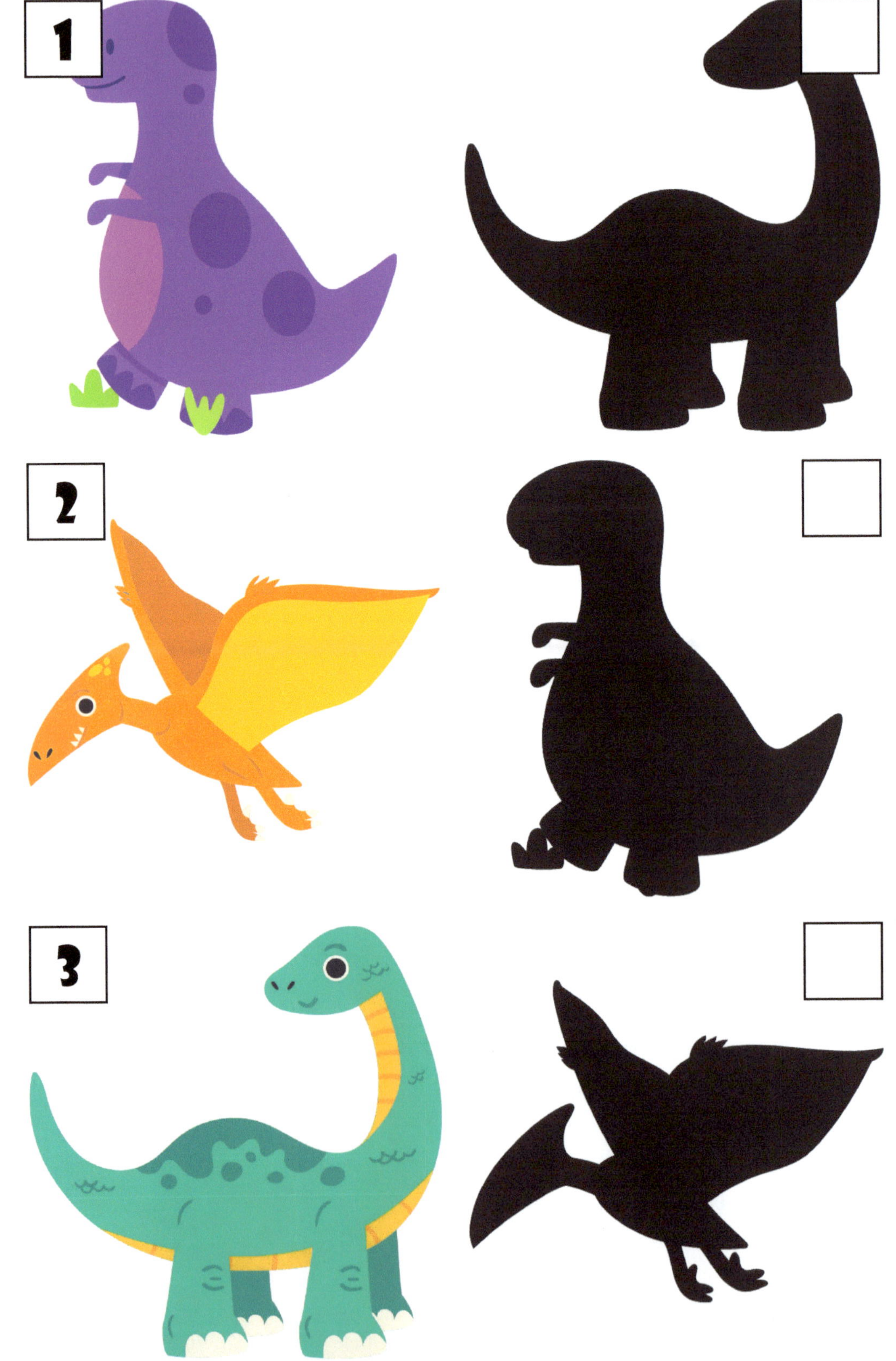

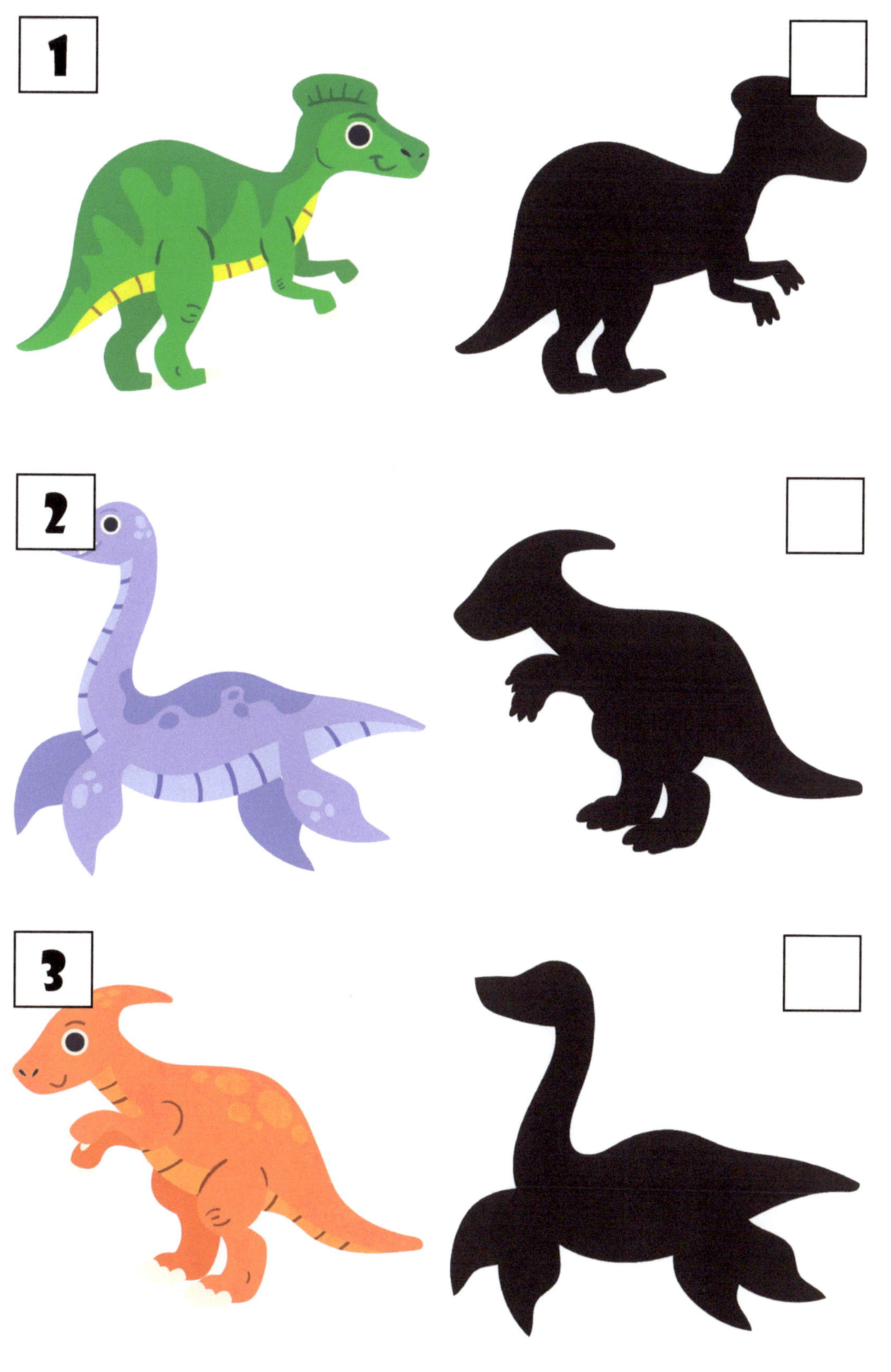

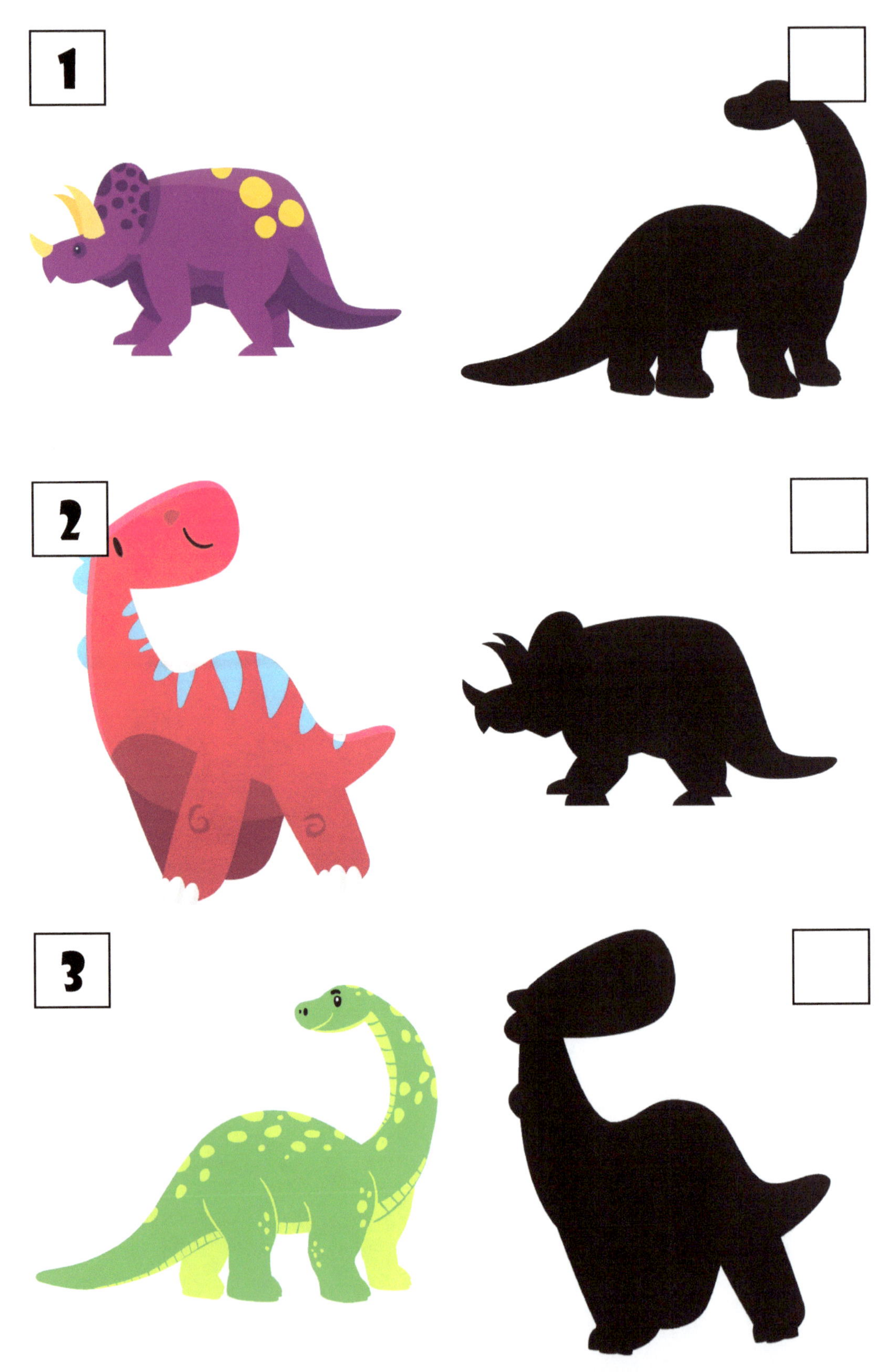

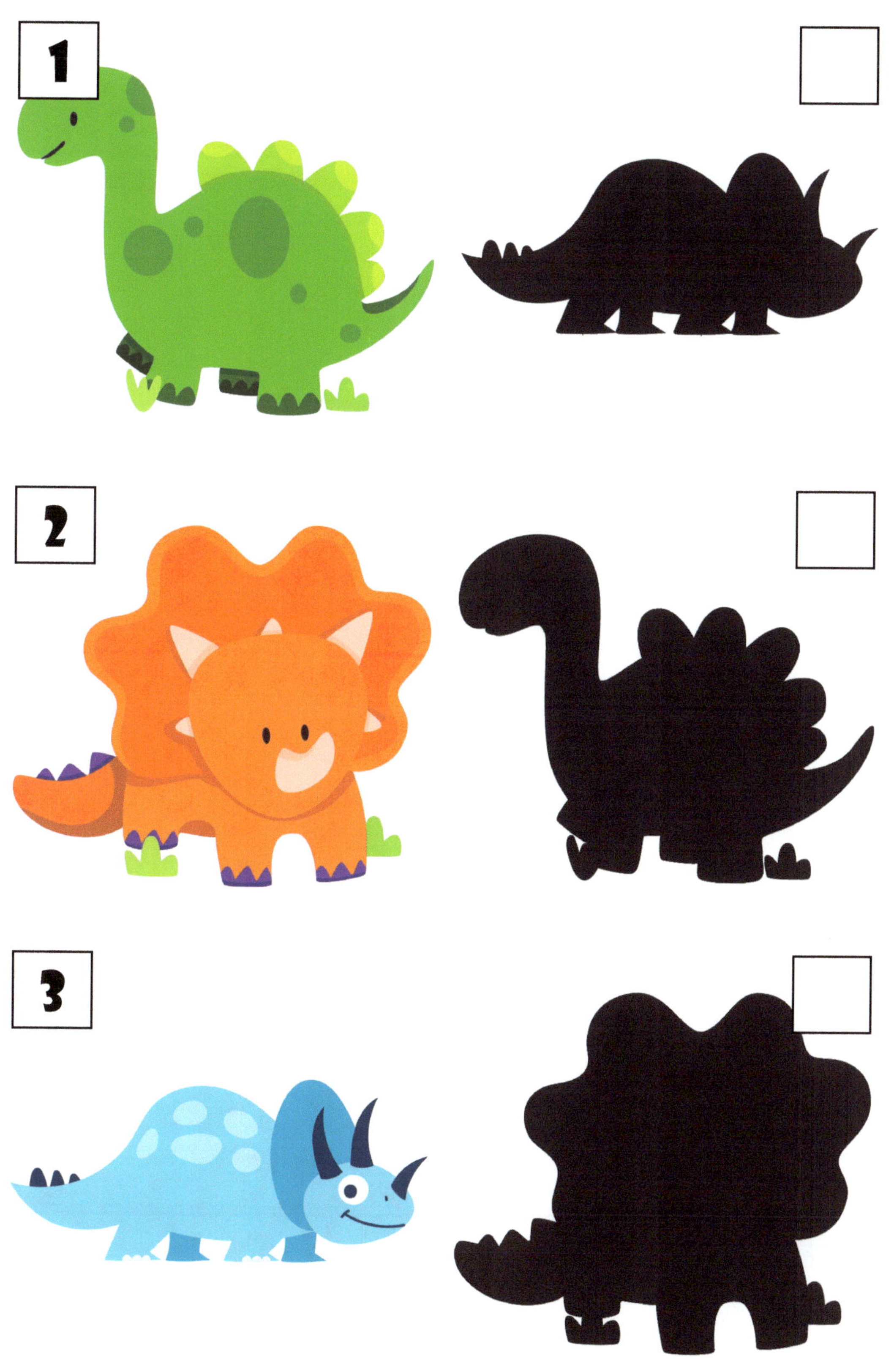

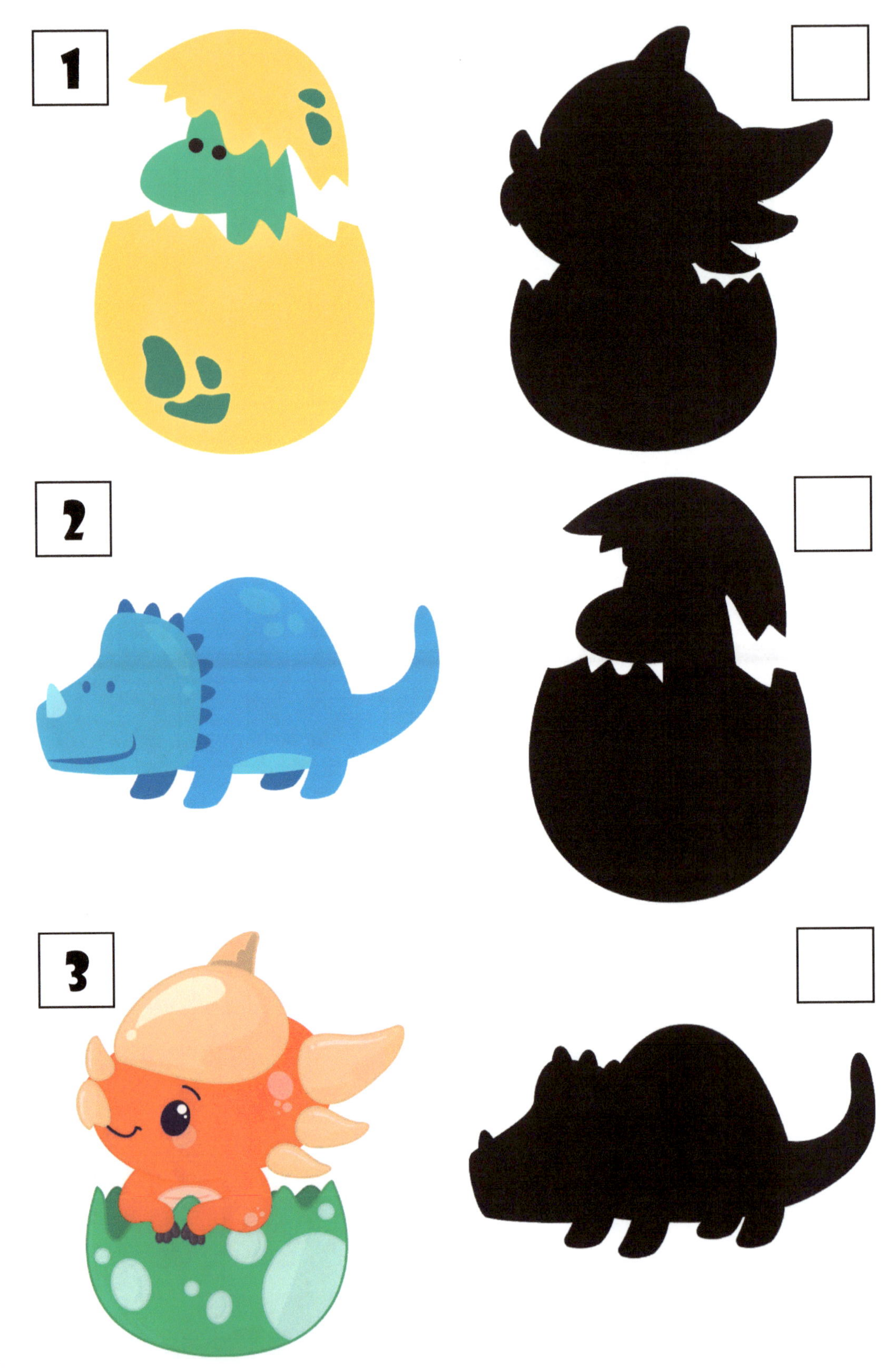